*O*f *B*enefit *t*o *O*neself *a*nd *O*thers:

A Critique of the Six Perfections

六波羅蜜自他兩利之評析

By Venerable Master Hsing Yun
Translated by John Balcom

©2002 Buddha's Light Publishing

By Venerable Master Hsing Yun
Translated by Professor Ph.D. John Balcom
Endnote by Fo Guang Shan
International Translation Center
Edited by Brenda Bolinger
Book and cover designed by Mei-Chi Shih

Published by Buddha's Light Publishing
3456 S. Glenmark Drive,
Hacienda Heights, CA 91745, U.S.A.
Tel: (626) 923-5143 / (626) 961-9697
Fax: (626) 923-5145 / (626) 369-1944
e-mail: itc@blia.org

ISBN: 0-9715612-6-5

Library of Congress Control Number: 2002100021

Contents

Acknowledgements

We received a lot of help from many people and we want to thank them for their efforts in making the publication of this book possible. We especially appreciate Venerable Tzu Jung, the Chief Executive of Fo Guang Shan International Translation Center (F.G.S.I.T.C.), Venerable Hui Chuan, the Abbot of Hsi Lai Temple, and Venerable Yi Chao, the Director of F.G.S.I.T.C. for their support and leadership; Professor John Balcom for his translation; Brenda Bolinger for her editing; Bill Maher, Echo Tsai, Mu-tzen Hsu, Oscar Mauricio for their proofreading; Mei-Chi Shih for her book and cover design; Venerable Miao Han and Mae Chu, for preparing the manuscript for publication. Our appreciation also goes to everyone who has supported this project from its conception to its completion.

Foreword

"Of Benefit to Oneself and Others: A Critique of the Six Perfections" provides valuable insight into the Buddhist perspective on life. While Buddhism can trace its historical roots back over 2500 years, its history in the West has been far shorter. Master Hsin Yun has devoted his entire life to Buddhism. Born in Mainland China in 1927, he fled to Taiwan in 1949, determined to continue the growth and development of Buddhism. In 1967 he founded Fo Guang Shan, which is dedicated to propagating education, culture and charity. Since that time, Fo Guang Shan has evolved into an international network of temples, monasteries, universities, relief agencies and Buddhist organizations and institutions too numerous to count.

Despite the size of these endeavors, Master Hsing Yun continues to follow the Buddhist tradition of teaching the Dharma personally. He has lectured and written extensively. Recent works include "Between Ignorance and Enlightenment," a column that appears in the Merit Times and provides observations on the beauty of applying a Buddhist perspective to daily life.

He has also promoted inter-faith understanding and cooperation. Buddhism does not require an individual to follow a system of thought and practices that he or she cannot understand; rather, it presents a perspective on life that is based on cause and effect and dependent origination; an individual does not follow Buddhism simply out of blind faith. Instead, the individual is persuaded (or not) by the logic of a teacher, the scriptures, and his or her own personal experience. "Of Benefit to Oneself and Others: A Critique of the Six Perfections" presents logical reasons why striving to follow Buddhism's six perfections are not merely a moral or ethical necessity designed to benefit others, but rather why following them is necessary in order for a person to improve his or her own personal life. In so doing, Master Hsing Yun is able to help the reader sees beyond the illusions of self and other and to glimpse the sameness and unity that is beyond the illusory world that we commonly live in.

Tom Manzo, Ph.D.
Foreign Languages
San Antonio College
San Antonio, Texas.

About
Venerable Master Hsing Yun

Venerable Master Hsing Yun was born in Jiangdu, Jiangsu province, China, in 1927. Tonsured under Venerable Master Zhikai at age twelve, he became a novice monk at Qixia Vihara School and Jiaoshan Buddhist College. He was fully ordained in 1941, and is the 48th Patriarch of the Linji (Rinzai) Chan school.

He went to Taiwan in 1949 where he undertook to revitalizing Chinese Mahayana Buddhism on the island with a range of activities novel for its time. In 1967, he founded the Fo Guang Shan (Buddha's Light Mountain) Buddhist Order, and had since established more than a hundred temples in Taiwan and on every continent worldwide. Hsi Lai Temple, the United States Headquarters, was built outside Los Angeles in 1988.

At present , there are nearly two thousand monks and nuns in the Fo Guang Shan Buddhist

Order. The organization also oversees sixteen Buddhist colleges; four publishing houses including, Buddha's Light Publishing, Hsi Lai University Press; four universities, one of which is Hsi Lai University in Los Angeles; a secondary school; a satellite television station; an orphanage; and a nursing home for the elderly.

A prolific writer and an inspiring speaker, Master Hsing Yun has written many books on Buddhist sutras and a wide spectrum of topics over the past five decades. Most of his speeches and lectures were compiled into essays defining Humanistic Buddhism and outlining its practice. Some of his writings and lectures are translated into different languages, such as English, Spanish, German, Russian, Japanese, Korean, etc.

The Venerable Master is also the founder of Buddha's Light International Association, a worldwide organization of lay Buddhists dedicated to the propagation of Buddhism, with over 130 chapters and more than a million in membership.

*I*ntroduction

Buddhism is one of the world's major religions. But most religions see the universe and everything in it as deriving directly from a single omnipotent force. Buddhism, on the other hand, sees the universe and everything in it as arising from dependent origination[1]. Life and the cosmos are cyclical, having "no beginning or end and no inside or outside." The adherents of other religions hope and pray that the gods will grant them good health, long life, happiness, status, wealth, and many children and grandchildren. This hunger for gratification via an external source is a human weakness that can easily develop into superstition, attachment, and greed, in turn leading to a poverty of the spirit and the mind. But Buddhism is a religion that stresses "dependent origination and cause and effect." The Buddhist faith is founded on understanding and wisdom. For it is through the unfolding of wisdom that the original mind is recovered, unlocking its resources to fathom all principles such as the dependent origination of arising and extinction, and thereby allowing one to awake from ignorance and attain liberation, finding nirvana[2] in samsara[3], and establishing a happy life free from delusion. Thus, Buddhism advocates attaining liberation through one's own conduct.

Buddhism emphasizes that one treat others with selfless compassion, that one cultivate oneself through suffering loss and giving charity, that one be ever mindful of making sacrifices and contributions, and that one broadly form good affinities. In suffering losses, forming affinities, and benefiting others, a person is actually fostering his or her own conditions of blessings and morality, and accumulating the capital for future sage-hood. Where there is a cause, there is an effect, such as by liberating oneself one can liberate others and by liberating others one can save oneself.

In Buddhist belief there is no omnipotent force, no judge who rewards good and punishes evil. All fortune, good and bad, is determined by a person's own behavior. The Buddha is a model of equality and reason, a fine physician and guide, and not some supreme deity. The Dharma is the Law of Cause and Effect and karmic retribution, of reaping as one sows. There is no controlling force beyond cause and effect and the karma produced by a person's own behavior. We are our own god.

Regrettably, most people have not been able to investigate the teachings of Buddhism in any depth; instead, their understanding and beliefs are based on superficial appearances. Most people agree that Buddhism teaches that we should take delight in giving charity, govern ourselves by upholding the precepts, patiently bear all insults, never relax in our efforts, and sit long in meditation. Unfortunately, the practicality of these ideals in daily life is not always understood. However, Mahayana Buddhism teaches the applicability of the following six perfections[4]:

1. Giving charity. Is it for oneself or is it for others? It appears to be for others, but it is actually for oneself. Giving charity can liberate a person from stinginess and greed, and lead to wealth.

2. Upholding the precepts. Is this some kind of restriction or is it freedom? It looks like restriction, but it is actually freedom. Upholding the precepts can liberate a person from harm and lead to safety.

3. Patience. Is it advantageous or disadvantageous? It looks disadvantageous, but it is actually advantageous. Patience can liberate a person from anger and lead to uprightness.

4. Diligence. Does this mean difficulty or happiness? It looks difficult, but it actually brings happiness. Diligence can liberate a person from laziness and lead to success.

5. Meditation. Is it something dull or is it lively? It looks dull, but it's lively. Contemplation can liberate a person from distraction and lead to serenity.

6. Prajna-wisdom. Is it to be sought outside or inside oneself? It looks like it must be sought without, but it must be sought within. Wisdom can liberate a person from ignorance and lead to the truth.

Judging from the implications of the six perfections described above, it would appear that the way of the bodhisattva is practiced for the benefit of others. Actually, it is also practiced for the benefit of oneself. Now let us look at the pros and cons of the six perfections and examine how they benefit both oneself and others.

*T*he Perfection of Giving Charity:

Of Benefit to Oneself and Others

When Buddhism speaks of giving charity, it means giving to others with a compassionate mind. This means giving one's share in everything to others. In this world, it is those who know how to give to others who are the richest. By the same token, those who only look to take from others are the poorest. This is because giving is like the sowing of seed. If seed is not sown, how can there be a harvest? If one doesn't give to others, how can one ever become rich? Nagarjuna's[5] *Treatise on the Perfection of Great Wisdom (Mahaprajnaparamita Sastra)*[6] says as much: "Most people know that if you want cool shade, flowers, and fruit, you have to plant trees. Giving is the same. Giving is a must if you want peace, happiness, liberation from suffering in this life and the next, and the fruit of unsurpassed perfect wisdom."

Giving charity is also like cash savings. Most people, when they have some money, want to put it in the bank. According to the *Precepts of the Mulasarvastivada School* (*Mulasarvastivada Vinaya*),[7] "Accumulated wealth and riches will be dispersed; fame and high status will see a fall." In this impermanent world, everything goes through the process of forming, abiding, decaying, and extinguishing. Even banks can go broke. "All the world's wealth is possessed by five groups[8]" (*Collection of Great Treasures* [*Maharatnakuta Sutra*]).[9] People could count themselves fortunate if they didn't encounter corrupt officials, if they didn't have unfilial children and grandchildren, and if they never encounter fire, flood, or thieves. We enter this world empty handed, and leave it the same way. Even if we possess great wealth, when we die, we can't take anything with us except karma. For this reason, understanding the merits of giving charity is the surest way to manage one's money.

A gatha says: "For each grain that falls to the ground, one hundred are harvested; for each coin given in charity, ten thousand will return; deposit it in a strong storehouse, and your children and grandchildren will enjoy it without end." Giving charity is the securest of treasuries, one that, due to cause and effect, cannot be robbed. Thus, wealth is a result of merit, while the ability to use it is wisdom. Only when a person knows how to give charity is the money indeed theirs.

All good deeds come down to giving charity. Giving charity results in merits, and it is the person who gives charity that is happy and wise. Emperor Wu of the Liang Dynasty once served in a temple before his ascension to the throne. During one of his past lives as a woodcutter, he decided to give charity. Much later he enjoyed the merit of royalty. Hence the parable: "Cultivating merit is easy with the Triple Gem. For each coin given in charity ten thousand will return. If you don't believe it, just look at Emperor Wu of the Liang Dynasty. He once gave a bamboo hat in charity and later received the empire."

Giving charity is the manifestation of compassion, and it builds good affinities. To understand the benefits of giving charity just look at our daily life. When we water flowers and fruit trees, they will be all the more green and lush, providing people with enjoyment. If we provide a fierce beast with food, it will be grateful, hence the examples of a python requiting kindness, or a dog rescuing its master.

Besides material giving, the scriptures also speak of many types of charity, including "the giving of the Dharma" and "the giving of *abhaya*[10]." Skill, knowledge, and reason are examples of the former, while defending public welfare and justice, aiding the weak, fearlessly striving to help the needy, and relieving the distressed are all examples of the latter. Moreover, even a good word, a smile, a parade salute, a friendly bringing together of the palms, and a nod are also forms of giving charity.

But superficially, giving charity appears to mean that I must give to others. It's easy for most people to give something to themselves, but giving to others is a different story. It is hard to give to others and this is what makes it difficult to purely practice the Dharma or to part with wealth. By saying that "it appears to be for others, but actually it is for oneself" makes it a little easier to perform acts of charity.

Giving is the first step in caring for sentient beings and also the basis for the liberation of sentient beings. When a person is so poor that he is hungry, poorly clothed, and too weak to do anything, he must be provided with food, clothing, and other daily necessities through giving. Once he is clothed and fed, then he will have the energy needed for other pursuits. This is what is meant by the words, "First tempt him with desire, then lead him to the Buddha's wisdom" (*Lotus Sutra* [*Saddharmapundarika Sutra*]).[11] Thus, the first five of the six perfections including giving charity are skillful means. But only with prajna, or wisdom, the sixth perfection, will the six perfections become the Dharma of the Mahayana bodhisattva path. Lacking prajnaparamita, or the perfection of wisdom, will make the other perfections conditioned dharmas[12], not the unconditioned dharmas[13] of the bodhisattva path.

Any person with a heart can perform an act of giving. But giving without wisdom can result in haggling, inflexibility, and distinctions such as "superior" and "inferior," and as a consequence, acts of giving will have form, which is not in accordance with the Dharma. Examples would include giving charity to enhance one's reputation, giving charity to earn praise or repayment, giving for the sake of pride, regrets in giving, unwillingness to give, and giving inappropriately[14] (*Sutra on the Principles of the Six Paramitas*).[15] Therefore, the best type of giving is one that is without attachment to form, which means "making no distinctions between giver and recipient and the essential emptiness of giver, receiver, and gift."

Giving charity not only helps others, but also can liberate oneself from the fundamental afflictions of stinginess and greed. The *Rain of Treasures Sutra*[16] says, "Giving allows one to cut off the three unwholesome conditions—avariciousness, jealousy, and bad thoughts." People suffer from afflictions because of the three poisons—greed, hatred, and

ignorance. And of these, greed is the most fundamental. The *Merits of Right Deeds Sutra*[17] says,
"When greed arises in the heart, it is like a person
bound and enslaved. But greed is a bad habit com-
mon to all sentient beings. For example, after three
meals, some people want more to eat; when a person
sees something nice, they want it; when a person has
loads of money, they want more. Greed leads to a
falling out between father and son and creates con-
flicts among brothers. Examples are commonplace
these days. Giving charity is the best moral practice
for ridding oneself of greed and helping others; giving charity is the best way to cultivate merit. Those
who are stingy and greedy should practice giving."

Initially, practicing giving seems difficult.
But once a person understands how giving aids others, and can treat others as he would himself, promot-
ing good causes and good karma, practicing giving
will be possible despite the difficulties. Why not try
it if it will increase the success of a person's self-cultivation?

Therefore, true givers not only give to others, but also to themselves. For in Buddhism, there is no difference among the giver, the receiver, and the merit. The giver of charity ought to thank the recipient of charity for accepting the good causes of his charity and even "give without the distinctions of giver and recipient and of the essential emptiness of giver, receiver, and gift." Only then can it really be called the perfection of giving charity.

If a person expects repayment or hopes to earn praise for their gifts of charity, it is still greed and cannot be called "joyful giving." Giving joyfully is very important when giving charity. In the sutras, the banyan tree is an example of joyfully giving charity and the merit it accrues, for from a single seed grows a tree covered with fruit. Therefore, the benefits of giving charity are described as "sowing one and harvesting ten" and "sowing ten and harvesting one hundred."

Additionally, according to the scriptures, the fruits of giving vary with the charity that is given.

For example, giving clothes will be rewarded with a fine complexion, giving food will be rewarded with great strength, giving a lamp will be rewarded with clear vision, giving a ride will be rewarded with peace and happiness, and giving lodging will be rewarded with having no wants (*Sutra on Upasaka Precepts* [*Upasakasila Sutra*]).[18]

According to another scripture, giving flowers enables one to fully enjoy the seven limbs of enlightenment;[19] giving incense will leave one's body scented with the fragrance of the precepts, concentration, and wisdom; giving fruit will produce the fruit of no outflows;[20] giving food will give one longevity, eloquence, dignified appearance, strength, and happiness; giving clothing will bring one the appearance of purity and modesty; giving a lamp will allow one to accomplish the Buddha's eye, illuminating the nature of all phenomena; giving a ride will bestow one with the most supreme supernatural powers; giving ornamental adornments will enhance one with the eighty accessory marks;[21] giving precious jewels will enrich one with the thirty-two excellent marks of a

Buddha;[22] giving physical efforts will endow one with the ten powers (*bala*) of the Tathagata[23] and the four grounds of self-confidence (*vaisaradya*)[24] (*Treatise on Arising the Mind of Enlightenment*).[25]

And from yet another source, giving food and drink will bring strength, dignified appearance, longevity, happiness, and respect; giving clothing will give a sense of modesty, virtue, righteousness, and peace of body and mind; giving lodging will provide the seven-treasure palace where the five sense-desires will be satisfied; giving fluid one will satisfy the five sense-desires, and never know hunger or thirst; giving bridges, boats, and all sorts of footwear one will have all modes of transportation in life; giving parks one will be regarded with high esteem and be viewed as most reliable by all sentient beings (*Treatise on the Perfection of Great Wisdom*).

But a discussion of the value of giving charity cannot be limited to the quantity and size of the gift. Other fine gifts of charity include: helping others, saying a good word, teaching the Dharma, pious devotion, rejoicing in the wholesome deeds of others, and the like. In giving charity, "When our intentions differ, so do the fruits." Sometimes, a small gift of giving might bear great fruits. The poor girl and the coin is one example. In this instance, a poor girl offered a small coin to the Buddha and was subsequently rewarded with the good fortune of being an empress. If a bit of bread is given with all one's heart, wishing that all hunger might be wiped out, the merit of such a wish will be bountiful. If "a poor person joyfully observes someone's giving, the joy they experience will bring merit to match the giver's" (*Sutra of Cause and Effect*).[26]

From the forgoing it is clear that giving charity is not necessarily dependent upon money and wealth. The mind to give is more important; but intentions are the most important. Some forms of giving have form, and are performed for merit; but the heart's intent is without structure, without form, and without condition. Naturally, the merit accrued from such giving will be boundless and endless.

In short, there are many types of giving. Specifically: respect for others, words of encouragement, a polite smile, teaching a skill, psychological guidance, and the like are all excellent forms of giving. As the scriptures say, "The best of all offerings is an offering of the Dharma." Anyone can offer riches, but few are those who can offer the Dharma. For this reason, "Charity is easy, but culture and education are difficult." If one can elevate charity from giving riches to giving the Dharma, so much greater will be the benefits to oneself and others. This is because there are five remarkable and outstanding things about giving the Dharma as charity:

1. Giving the Dharma profoundly benefits oneself and others, giving riches does not.

2. Giving the Dharma will allow sentient beings to be born outside the three realms,[27] but giving riches will not allow birth beyond the realm of sense-desire.

3. Giving the Dharma will purify the Dharmakaya, but giving riches will only increase outward appearances.

4. Giving the Dharma is without limit, but riches have an end.

5. Giving the Dharma can eliminate ignorance, but giving riches can only stifle greed (*Sutra of Golden Light* [*Suvarnaprabhasa Sutra*]).[28]

The *Sutra on the Perfection of Giving* (*Dana-paramita Sutra*) says that people are poor because they were stingy in their previous lives; the rich are so because they enjoyed giving charity in a past life. For this reason, giving charity appears to mean giving to others, but the person who really benefits is one-self. Giving charity is like sowing seed; if it is not sown in a field, how can there be a harvest? If the seed is sown, there will be a harvest. The time will be determined by when causes and conditions ripen.

In summary, is charity for others or for one-self? The concept of "being willing to part with things" is significant, because a person receives only by giving. Giving is not simply a way to assist others; it is also a way for a person to enhance their own life. Therefore, there can be no doubt that giving benefits oneself and others.

The Perfection of Upholding the Precepts:
Freedom or Restriction?

Upholding the precepts is an important issue when it comes to the study and practice of Buddhism. The precepts are the standard for behavior with regard to body, speech, and mind. It would be chaos without rules: without the direction of rules, people would run wild in body and mind. The precepts offer moral guidance for us and can lead us to the path of liberation. The *Sutra of the Teachings Bequeathed by the Buddha*[29] says: "The precepts are the true basis for liberation." The sutra also says, "The precepts should be our guide."

The precepts are like the law or school rules. Upholding the precepts is like obeying the law and observing the rules. When people break the law, the law will punish them; when people violate the precepts, the law of cause and effect will punish them. For this reason, it is not only Buddhists who would benefit from upholding the precepts. All people should uphold the precepts just as all people should obey the law. The reason being that upholding the precepts is the basis for proper conduct.

The law of the land and even school rules set a passive norm for good behavior for oneself. But the advice of Buddhist precepts—"do no evil; do all good" (*Gatha of the Seven Ancient Buddhas*),[30] does not just passively counter the false and prohibit evil and set a standard, but also demand the active cultivation of virtue along with doing good and benefiting others. The *Sutra of the Bodhisattva Stages* [*Bodhisattvabhumi Sutra*][31] says, "Those who uphold the precepts will feel no regard for hatred but will always encounter joy. They will also enjoy mindfulness that benefits themselves, which is called self-mindfulness; furthermore, because of their self-discipline, other sentient beings will not fear them, which is called benefiting others." Upholding the precepts is the Mahayana way of benefiting others by benefiting oneself, and leads us on the all-important path to liberation.

But Buddhist precepts emphasize liberating others, and even if taking action to save others means shouldering the cause and effect of this responsibility, one need not be afraid. That's why there is the example of "slaying one to save a hundred"[32] from the time when the Buddha was cultivating the bodhisattva path. Such an example indicates that the Buddhist precepts amount to more than simply doing no evil in a passive fashion, but also actively trying to liberate others.

While the Buddhist precepts are exceedingly accommodating, repentance for committing *parajika*[33] is impossible. However, there is a lot of room for repentance for violating all other precepts. Most people are afraid to violate the precepts, so they don't dare vow to uphold them. Actually, if people violates the precepts after vowing to uphold them, all they need to do is be repentant and they will be liberated. If a person doesn't vow to uphold the precepts, it doesn't mean there will be no karmic retribution for violating them; but if a person has made this vow and sincerely repents violating them, then the bad karma will be lessened. The Buddhist scriptures compare bad karma to a stone and repentance to a Dharma boat; with the Dharma boat of repentance, the stones of bad karma can be carried without sinking the boat. Most people believe that they can do whatever they want if they don't vow to uphold the precepts, because they can't violate them if they don't make this vow in the first place. This is the wrong view. Broken precepts can be repented, but wrong views cannot.

In Buddhism, a person who violates the precepts is not necessarily disgraced—all he needs to do is be sincerely repentant and there is hope for turning over a new leaf. But a person who holds wrong views is like someone with an incurable illness. Violating the precepts is an error in behavior, whereas wrong views are basically an error in thought. An error in behavior can be corrected, but with a basic error in thought, the mind will always be impervious to truth. It is better for a person to vow to uphold the precepts and then violate them than to refuse to make this vow and then violate them. Why? Because "If someone knows they have done wrong and are repentant, good roots will increase" (*Five Part Vinaya [Mahisasaka Vinaya]*).[34]

Of the three studies—precepts, concentration, and wisdom; upholding the precepts is the foremost, because only then can one meditate, and only through meditation can wisdom be revealed, and only with wisdom can one avoid sinking into the sea of suffering. For this reason, "Upholding the precepts is the unsurpassable basis for bodhi" (*Flower Ornament Scripture [Avatamsaka Sutra]*).[35] Upholding the precepts is one path to liberation. But seeking liberation without vowing to uphold the precepts is as the Treatise on the Perfection of Great Wisdom says, "Like trying to walk without feet, fly without wings, ford a river without a boat. It's impossible." Seeking good effects without upholding the precepts is the same.

There are references to the advantages and benefits of upholding the precepts throughout the scriptures. For example:

"There are five merits to upholding the precepts. First, everything sought will always be realized according to one's wishes. Second, wealth will increase and not decrease. Third, one will be revered and loved by all. Fourth, a person will have a good reputation and be renowned. Fifth, a person will be reborn in heaven after he/she dies" (*Long Discourses of the Buddha* [*Dirghagama*]).[36]

"Those who receive the five precepts are blessed and [people will] not fear [them]" (*Sutra Concerning Auspicious and Inauspicious* [*Conducts*] *Requested by Ananda*).[37]

"If people uphold the five precepts, the twenty-five celestial guardians who protect each of them to the left and right and above the doors of their dwellings will make all things lucky" (*Abhisecana Sutra as Discoursed by the Buddha* [*Mahabhise-kamantra Sutra*]).[38]

"If people uphold the precepts with purity, they will possess the good Dharma. Without upholding precepts with purity, no merits will accrue. That is why the precepts are the first seat of peace and merit" (*Sutra of the Teachings Bequeathed by the Buddha*).

"If people are compassionate and do not kill, they will obtain five blessings. First, long life; second, well-being; third, they will not be harmed by war, wild animals, or poisonous insects; fourth, eternal life in heaven; fifth, long life if they descend from heaven to be born on earth" (*Sutra on the Origins of Wholesomeness and Unwholesomeness*).[39]

"If people do not steal, five faiths will be theirs. They will have great wealth that can't be taken away by government officials, flood, fire, bandits, enemies, or prodigal children. They will be revered and loved by all. Wherever they go, all will be calm and they will encounter no difficulties nor have any fears. This wealth will be saved and given wisely in charity" (*Sutra of the Sea Dragon King* [*Sagaranagarajapariprccha Sutra*]).[40]

"People who do not slander, revile, or spread rumors about others will obtain five good things. One, their word will be believed; two, they will be beloved by all; three, their breath will smell good; four, they will be reborn in heaven and respected by all; five, when reborn on earth, they will endowed with complete dentition[41]" (*Sutra on the Origins of Wholesomeness and Unwholesomeness*).

The benefits to be derived from upholding the precepts are measureless. But most people don't understand this. They think that they will be subject to too many limits and restrictions if they vow to uphold the precepts and therefore they dare not. Actually, upholding the precepts is freedom and true liberation, because the collective meaning of the precepts is not infringing upon the rights of others. Not killing means not violating someone else's body; not stealing means not taking someone else's wealth; not engaging in sexual misconduct means practicing chastity and not violating someone else's body; not lying means not slandering someone else or destroying their trust; not taking intoxicants means not violating one's own wisdom and safety.

Therefore, if everyone upholds the precepts and respects everyone else's rights, then each person's life, wealth, home, job, and reputation will all be ensured. But if a person does not uphold the precepts and kills, steals, engages in sexual misconduct, lies, and uses intoxicants, then not only will others be harmed, but that person himself will wind up in jail; all his freedom lost. Thus, upholding the precepts means "freedom for oneself; freedom for others; freedom for all." If one person in a country upholds the precepts, then one person is sound; if one household upholds the precepts, then one household is sound; if an entire society's people uphold the precepts, then that society will be stable. The *Ritual of the Triple Gem Refuge and Five Precepts Ceremony* (*Sanqui Wujie Zheng Fan*)[42] says, "If ten people in a village of one hundred families uphold the five precepts, the ten people will be pure; if one hundred people in a state of a thousand households cultivate the 'ten wholesome conducts[43],' then one hundred people will be on friendly terms; if this teaching is spread to a thousand households, then the benevolent will number in the thousands. By practicing one virtue, one evil is eliminated; if one evil is eliminated, then so is one punishment; if one punishment is eliminated, then ten thousand punishments within a state can be done away with. This is called creating peace without striving for it."

For this reason, one might ask what help or contribution might Buddhism offer to the state? If the hearts of the people are purified with the five precepts, then precautions are taken against crimes before they happen, obviating the need for punishment by law. This is why Dr. Sun Yat-sen said, "Buddhism is benevolence that can save the world, and it can supplement the insufficiencies of the law."

If behavioral scientists were to go to prisons today and investigate, they would find that those deprived of their freedom had violated the five precepts in some manner. People inevitably lose their freedom for killing, disfiguration, assault, and unpremeditated murder. People can be imprisoned and lose their freedom for stealing, robbing, embezzlement, burglary, blackmail, and kidnapping. People can be locked up and lose their freedom for sexual misconduct, rape, abduction, bigamy, indecent behavior, domestic abuse, and sexual harassment. Lying, slander, breach of contract, perjury, threatening, rumor mongering, and forgery can also lead to imprisonment. People will be subjected to punishment under the law for abusing drugs and alcohol, as well as dealing, trafficking, and manufacturing illicit drugs. Lastly, falsely claiming enlightenment is too wicked to be pardoned.

As such, there is no such thing as a person who achieves freedom and liberation without upholding the precepts. Violating the precepts means infringing upon the freedom of oneself and others. Killing is to infringe upon the freedom of others to live; stealing is to infringe upon the freedom of others to possess wealth; sexual misconduct is to infringe upon the bodily freedom of others; lying is to infringe upon the freedom of others to a reputation; using intoxicants is to infringe upon one's freedom to wisdom and health, and furthermore due to a loss of reason to infringe upon the freedom of others.

Therefore, Buddhists can obtain freedom and avoid restrictions only by upholding the precepts. This being the case, are the precepts restriction or liberation? The answer is clear.

The Perfection of Patience:

Between Weakness and Strength

Buddhism calls this world of ours the Saha, which means "patiently endure." People should have patience. To study and practice Buddhism with the aim of attaining Buddhahood requires patience.

Patience means enduring the insults of others without anger. Therefore, patience can be defined as enduring the physical and mental vexations and sufferings of this world without becoming angry, developing hatred, or harboring evil intentions or thoughts of revenge.

According to the *Biography of Sakyamuni (Buddhacarita Sutra)*,[44] in a past life, when the Buddha was cultivating the Way, he was once pursued and reviled by five hundred zealous men. Wherever the Buddha went, they followed him and reviled him. But the Buddha's attitude was like that described in the *Sutra on the Bodhisattva Precepts*, "Never becoming the least bit angry at others, [the bodhisattva] always examines the situation with compassion." As the *Sutra of Forty-Two Sections*[45] says, "What is the greatest strength? The patient are the most settled; they do not complain; they will certainly be honored among people." Likewise, the *Sutra of the Right Mindfulness on the Dharma (Saddharma-smrtyupasthana Sutra)*[46] says, "Those who are patient have the best hearts." And the *Sutra of the Teachings Bequeathed by the Buddha* says, "Patience is a virtue that surpasses upholding the precepts and practicing asceticism. Those who are capable of patience can be called strong and superior."

Patience is not necessarily weak or cowardly behavior that displays "not returning blow for blow or word for word." Patience is great courage, strength, fearlessness, and responsibility. If a person "cannot happily endure being reviled by others as if drinking sweet dew, then they cannot be counted among the wise" (*Sutra of the Teachings Bequeathed by the Buddha*). This being the case, patience is strength, responsibility, understanding, and it is praj-na-wisdom.

There are three levels of patience: patience of life, patience of dharma, and patience of non-arising dharmas. "Patience of life" means enduring life's joys and sorrows. It also means taking responsibility and doing what is right; it means properly handling what is right and wrong as well as not being affected by gain and loss; it means overcoming positive and negative emotions. Throughout life, if one is to live free, one must have patience of life. For example, to work or to get to the office, one must get up early and take the bus as well as endure traffic jams, hot and cold weather, a lack of sleep, among other discomforts, and even other human affairs where there are differences of opinion, love and hate. Throughout life, if a person just wants to go on living, patience is necessary. This is "patience of life," and it is a form of wisdom and strength that a person learns from staying engaged in daily living.

"Patience of dharma" means that in life we

must be able to restrain, mediate, and alter our habitual greed, hatred, and ignorance. It also means to endure the reality of all phenomena that arise and are extinguished due to dependent origination, and for one's mind to dwell at peace with this truth, unmoved by life and death. This means not only being unmoved by birth, old age, sickness, and death as well as by life's various emotions and desires, but also having true patience, knowledge, and the ability to handle, transform, and extinguish suffering. This is "patience of dharma." "Patience of dharma" is the awareness that "everything arises from causes and conditions and everything is essentially empty," the clear understanding of the principles of dependent origination and cause and effect, as well as the prajna-wisdom of human reason and emotion.

"Patience of non-arising dharmas" refers to the highest state of patience beyond unconscious patience. It is the awareness that, by nature, all dharmas do not arise nor are they extinguished, and that there is no patience or lack of patience, and that all dharmas are this way. The "patience of non-arising dharmas" is the suchness-wisdom that there is no origination and that sees all the unproduced dharmas. Patience is wisdom; it is an awareness of the universe and the human condition. It is the strength to accept, bear, take charge, transform, handle, and liberate. Not everything goes the way one wishes in life. Who does not often have to exercise patience? Endurance breeds strength! Therefore, the best solution to suffering a setback, being wronged, finding things hard to bear, or being slandered is patience. Knives, guns, poison, and cruelty are powerless against the strength of patience.

According to the *Gradual Discourses of the Buddha* (*Ekottarikagama*),[47] "A child's strength is in its tears, a woman's strength is in her charm, a king's strength is in his power and influence, an arhat's strength is in his paucity of desire, a monastic's strength is in patience, and a bodhisattva's strength is in compassion." Patience is strong, stable, and tempering. It takes a skilled hand to turn out a jade bracelet, and only a patient artist can produce a lasting work of art. Only when plum blossoms are cleansed by frost and snow will they be fragrant. If a person does not experience and patiently bear with life's difficulties, they will never truly be numbered among the outstanding. Mencius said, "That is why when heaven is going to place a great responsibility on a man, it will test his resolve, exhaust his body, make him suffer from hunger and hardship, and frustrate his efforts. In this way his patience and endurance are developed, and his weaknesses overcome." Clearly, if a person is to be successful, he must endure the unendurable and do the undoable.

The Buddha had ten great disciples. Among them, Sariputra was moved to give his eyes in charity, thus winning Heaven's favor. Aniruddha practiced so hard that he went blind. Later he was taught by the Buddha and obtained the "divine-eye." That's why according to the *Cultivating the Tree as the Bodhisattva's Practice Sutra*,[48] "Patience is the basis of practice for the bodhisattva; the strength of patience will lead to Buddhahood."

Anger, one of the three poisons, can be controlled with patience. According to the *Sutra of the Teachings Bequeathed by the Buddha*, "Anger is more like a fire raging in the mind. Prevent it and do not let it enter your mind. The worst thief of merit and virtue is anger." According to the *Garden of the Dharma and Pearl Forest (Fayuan Zhulin)*,[49] "Anger is the root of losing all good; it is the cause for starting on the path of evil." It goes on to say that it is "The enemy of Dharma joy; the thief of a good mind; the storehouse for all evil speech; and the axe of disaster." When the mind gives rise to anger, wisdom is shut out, the way the bright moon is covered by dark clouds. It is also like a huge fire that burns and consumes a forest. That's why the sutra says, "When hatred arises, the door to all hindrances opens," and "Anger is the fire in the mind that consumes the forest of merit."

As we study and practice Buddhism, we accumulate merit, but we can lose it all when we indulge in anger. That is what is meant by, "Cultivating oneself for kalpas is the cause for accumulating great merit; but it can be reduced to nothing by one burst of anger. That's why Venerable Master Hanshan said, "To practice the bodhisattva path requires patience to preserve a true mind."

There are benefits to patience. According to the *Sutra on the Perfection of Patience*, "By embracing patience and acting with loving-kindness, in life after life there will be no hate; a calm mind will never be harmed by the poisons. We can rely on nothing but patience in life in this universe; patience means peace and stability without disaster. ...Patience is a divine armor that soldiers cannot pierce. Patience is a great ship that can make difficult crossings. Patience is a good medicine that can benefit everyone's life." The *Treasury of Truth* (*Dhammapada*)[50] says, "He who holds back anger like a runaway cart, him I call a real driver; others are but holding the reins." That is why "If one hopes to benefit oneself, one will benefit others, so practice patience" (*Sutra of the Right Mindfulness on the Dharma*).

Most people think that having patience means to lose, to be bullied, to give in, that it is a form of cowardliness. Actually, it is just like being a porter. A weak porter can't carry very much, a slightly stronger porter a bit more, and a strong porter a lot. Therefore, to be able to bear and endure is strength. A truly strong person can bear glory and disgrace, blame and praise, gain and loss, bitterness and happiness. By enduring, one benefits beyond compare.

Therefore, only by being patient in life will one not be discouraged or perturbed in mind. Having patience means more than just swallowing insults to smooth things out. By having patience, incomparable merit is accrued.

Is patience beneficial or is it a sign of weakness? The answer is clear.

The Perfection of Diligence:

Suffering or Happiness?

Work requires vigor and diligence. Cultivation also requires vigor and diligence. But does diligence mean suffering or happiness?

If diligence were characterized as suffering, who would willingly apply themselves? But if diligence is characterized as a form of happiness, don't the implications and significance become greater? But if diligence is indeed characterized as suffering, yet portrayed as possessing of an even greater happiness, then it is even more just.

As the proverb says, "Even if gold flows in with the tide, you still have to get up early and pull it out of the water." There's no such thing as a free lunch. "You shall reap as you sow." Such is the ineluctable Law of Cause and Effect.

The scholars and exam candidates of classical China "lived poor and were ignored for years, but once they passed the exam their renown spread across the empire." This was a result of diligence. The Buddha once told his disciples, "With diligence nothing is difficult. It is like a little stream that by its continuous flow can wear through a stone" (*Commentary on the Sutra of the Teachings Bequeathed by the Buddha*).[51]

What is the meaning of the Chinese compound 精進 (*jingjin*, or 'diligence')? In essence, 精 means pure and unmixed; 進 means going forward and never turning back. According to the teachings of Buddhism, this means that in the process of cultivating the good and cutting off evil, in eliminating the impure for the pure, a person devotes themselves wholeheartedly without slackening off, overcoming all difficulties to reach their goal. This is called diligence.

Diligence can universally inspire all kinds of good and all the corresponding merits. Although diligence is the fourth perfection, without it the others are impossible. This is because "Diligence is the driving force behind all good, and it produces good conduct according to the truth, including *anuttarasamyaksambodhi* (full enlightenment)" (*Treatise on the Perfection of Great Wisdom*). Clearly, diligence is the basis of cultivation.

It is right diligence only if it is proper and beneficial to our behavior. The sutras list four types of right diligence: the diligence that produces good where there is none; the diligence that increases existing good; the diligence that prevents evil where there is none; and the diligence that decreases evil where it already exists (*Treatise on Arising the Mind of Enlightenment*). If a bodhisattva lacks these four types of diligence, then the perfection of diligence cannot be realized.

Diligence is used to combat laziness. "If a lay Buddhist is lazy, he will have no clothes or food and be unsuccessful; if a monastic is lazy, he cannot extricate himself from the sufferings of samsara. All matters require diligence" (*Sutra on the Bodhisattva's Practice as Discoursed by the Buddha*).[52] Laziness is the accumulation of trouble; it is an illness. If one is lazy at home, one loses all mundane benefits; if one is lazy as a monastic, one loses all Dharma treasure. For this reason, laziness must be combated with diligence if there is to be wisdom.

Diligence is divided into diligence of the mind, which means cutting off unwholesomeness such as greed, anger, and affliction, and diligence of the body, which means broadly cultivating all good dharmas. According to the *Gradual Discourses of the Buddha*, Maitreya and the Buddha were cultivating at the same time. But because the Buddha courageously devoted himself to self-cultivation with diligence, he was the first to achieve Buddhahood. This is why the Buddha once told Ananda, "Diligence in the home brings a plenitude of food, clothing, and success, and the admiration of all; with diligence in the monastery practicing the Dharma will be accomplished. To achieve the thirty-seven wings of enlightenment (*bodhipaksika*),[53] samadhi, the treasury of Dharma, the cessation of transmigration, arrival at the other shore, and peace and happiness, one must practice diligently."

Additionally, the *Moon Lamp Samadhi Sutra* (*Samadhirajachandrapradipa Sutra*)[54] says that there are ten benefits to diligence: "1) A person will not be subdued by difficulties; 2) a person will receive the assistance of the Buddha; 3) a person will be protected by all guardians; 4) a person will hear the Dharma and not forget it; 5) a person will hear what has not been heard; 6) a person will become more eloquent; 7) a person will attain samadhi; 8) a person will seldom be ill or vexed; 9) a person will always digest what has been eaten; 10) the blue lotus (*utpala*) is different from a log.[55]"

The benefits of diligence are not limited to curing laziness but also to actualizing enlightenment. Diligence on the job means success; diligence in practicing the Dharma means merit; diligence in this life means certain success in the next. But most people look upon diligence as suffering and upon work and self-cultivation as perilous undertakings. But what kind of success will a person have if they don't diligently work and cultivate themselves? The long path of Buddhism can be traveled to the end only if one has diligence. The path of diligence requires:

1. Diligently devoting oneself to keeping in mind the suffering of all sentient beings. As Srimala vows, "From this day hence, and even to the day of attaining Buddhahood, if I see the lonely, the ill, or any other suffering sentient being, I will not rest until I have comforted them, expounding to them the Dharma and liberating them from suffering; only then will I rest" (*Lion's Roar of Queen Srimala Sutra* [*Srimalasimhanada Sutra*]).[56] With such a compassionate vow to keep the suffering of all sentient beings in mind, naturally she would be able to fulfill bodhi and cultivate herself with diligence.

2. Diligently devoting oneself to always maintaining the contemplation of impermanence. As the *Treatise on the Awakening of Faith in the*

Mahayana[57] says, "All conditioned phenomena in
the world are impermanent and subject to change
and destruction; all activities of the mind arise and
are extinguished from moment to moment; and all of
this induces suffering. One should contemplate that
all that had been in the past was as hazy as a dream,
that all that is at the moment is like a flash of light-
ning, and that all that will be in the future will be like
suddenly arising clouds.

Laziness generally stems from the attitude of
wanting to put off until tomorrow what we can do
today. This always leads to failure. But if we are
mindful that life is as described in Samantabhadra's[58]
Gatha of Warning for All Sentient Beings, which
says, "Life grows shorter with each passing day,"
then will any of us be lazy? Will any of us not give
rise to a mind of diligence?

What is not doable and attainable if we diligently give, uphold the precepts, have patience, contemplate, and cultivate wisdom?

Likewise, what is not doable or attainable if we diligently work, study, do good, and have initiative of mind?

Furthermore, what is not doable or attainable if we are diligently willing, compassionate, have a sense of modesty, and are zealous?

To awaken diligence in the mind, one must take it as a matter of extreme urgency. As such, we should cherish every moment and treasure time, just as Emperor Yu of the Xia Dynasty said, "Value not a piece of jade, but cherish every moment."

The Buddhas and bodhisattvas in the "three periods of time"[59] and "ten directions"[60] were able to perfect the Buddhist way because not one of them failed to feel the passage of time and not one of them failed to be tempered by hardship. That is why we have expressions such as, "Experiencing the bitterest hardship makes one stronger" and "Only after the chilling cold will the winter plum blossom be profusely fragrant."

A descendant of National Master Yulin, with the enforcement of the Emperor Yongzheng, detached himself and was finally enlightened[61]. Don't all these stories serve to demonstrate that if mundane or supramundane dharmas are to bear fruit diligence is necessary?

Avalokitesvara Bodhisattva traveled and taught in every country; Ksitigarbha Bodhisattva dwelled in hell to liberate sentient beings; patriarchs and masters have slaved on behalf of all sentient beings throughout history; all bodhisattvas have literally given all of themselves. They did so to fulfill great vows, and thus, reached a joyous realm.

Is diligence suffering or is it happiness? *Inspiration for the Bodhicitta Pledge*[62] says, "Momentary diligence in practice and cultivation leads to eternal happiness; being lazy for a lifetime will lead to future lives of suffering." How much suffering and happiness is to be found in diligence? Only the wise know.

The Perfection of Meditation:

Activity and Tranquility are One

"Everything can be accomplished if the mind is controlled." So says the *Sutra of the Teachings Bequeathed by the Buddha*. Everyday our minds are buffeted about by the five sense-desires and afflictions. The originally true mind of the Buddha Nature is obstructed by the false perceptions of the mind and consciousness. Therefore, although the Buddha stated that, "All people possess the Buddha Nature," the average person fails to manifest his Buddha Nature due to the obstructions of affliction. Only by stopping causes and conditions from arising and by stilling thoughts can the inherent wisdom possessed by all people be revealed, allowing a person to see their true mind and original nature, realize enlightenment, and become a Buddha. That is why Buddhism has always insisted that, "Focusing the mind accrues merit; a moment of distraction spells affliction."

Focusing the mind is called meditation. Meditation can be defined as the stilling of one's thoughts, or focusing the mind in one place and arriving at an attitude of stillness. The *Treatise on the Perfection of Great Wisdom* says that focusing a restless mind is called meditation. And a restless mind subject to distractions is as inconstant as smoke and clouds, and as flighty as a goose feather blown about in the air. It is as uncontrollable as a storm, and as capricious as a monkey on horseback. It is like muddy water and a dust covered mirror in which it is impossible to see one's face. Sadly, a restless mind will always keep us in samsara.

Meditation (concentration) is one of the three studies. Meditation and wisdom go hand in hand; the same can be said of 止(*zhi*) and 觀(*guan*). *Zhi* means stopping [delusion] or when the body and mind are still; *guan* is seeing [the truth], or when the mind is contemplating clearly. It will be difficult to attain Buddhahood by cultivating the bodhisattva path without equally practicing meditation and wisdom and cultivating *zhi* and *guan*. On the relationship between meditation and wisdom and zhi and guan, the *Sutra on the Principles of the Six Paramitas* has this to say: "Contemplation can lead to wisdom and wisdom in turn gives rise to meditation; meditation and wisdom are the basis for enlightenment to Buddhahood." And the *Treatise on the Completion of Truth (Satyasiddhi Sastra)*[63] says, "When the body and mind are still (*zhi*) the bonds of affliction can be untied, and when the mind sees clearly (*guan*) suffering can be eliminated; when the body and mind are still (*zhi*) it is like pulling grass with one's hands, and when the mind sees clearly (*guan*) it is like reaping with a sickle; when the body and mind are still (*zhi*) it is like sweeping the ground, and when the mind sees clearly (*guan*) it is like shoveling manure; when the body and mind are still (*zhi*) it is like scraping away filth, and when the mind sees clearly (*guan*) it is like washing with water."

Meditation is key to attaining Buddhahood. Most people do not understand the true significance of meditation. They think that Chan meditation means to sit cross-legged with the back ramrod straight, eyes focused on the nose, looking inward at the mind. As a result it is perceived to be as dry as dust and people fail to see what a lively part it plays in life. For example, during the Tang Dynasty Chan Master Longtan Chongxin asked Chan Master Daowu for instruction on how to practice. In reply, Chan Master Daowu said, "Bring me some tea and I drink for you. Bring me some food and I eat for you. Join your palms in a prayerful gesture and I nod to you. When has a single day gone by when I didn't diligently instruct you?"

Chan meditation is life. The chores of daily life such as carrying wood and water are all Chan meditation. Arching the brow and blinking the eyes are also Chan meditation. Drinking tea and eating are also subtleties of Chan meditation. Chan meditation is as lively as happy days. How can anyone think that Chan meditation is something for old monks and that it has nothing to do with life?

A student monk once asked Chan Master

Zhaozhou about the Way. The Master replied, "Have some tea!" Eating, bathing, and cleaning are all the Way. Through these, the Way and liberation can be attained, making exertions elsewhere unnecessary. The Sixth Patriarch exclaimed, "With an equanimous mind there is no need to arduously uphold the precepts; with righteous conduct, there is no need for insightful meditation." The deluded person is all talk, the wise act in mind; the road forward is the same for the sage and the commoner. Therefore, Chan doesn't necessarily discard life's sentiments. To put it clearly, Chan transcends the five sense-desires and the six dusts[64] with the intention of attaining a truer harmony and quietude.

The biggest mistake most people make is to separate work and practice. Chan Master Huangbo tilled the soil and planted vegetables; Chan Master Guishan fermented soybeans, made paste, and picked tea leaves; Chan Master Shishuang ground wheat and milled rice; Chan Master Linji planted pine trees and hoed the ground; Chan Master Xuefeng cut wood and carried water; others like Yangshan herded cattle and

Dongshan kept an orchard. In fact, these examples all demonstrate to us that Chan is part of life. If one does not lead an active life, how can one have active meditation?

Chan is natural; it is coexistent with nature. Chan does not conceal anything. With Chan, a person still wears clothes and eats. Seen with the eye of wisdom, expressions such as "Willful and at ease, acting as the situation dictates, free from worry, doing one's utmost in this world; no other explanation can describe Chan better," and "The jade green bamboo leaves are prajna-wisdom; the lush yellow flowers are all wonderful truth" indicate that everything is Chan. Before enlightenment, a mountain appears to be a mountain, and water, water. After attaining enlightenment, the mountain still appears to be a mountain and water, water. But the mountain and the water before and after enlightenment are two different things. After enlightenment, we coexist and are of oneness - we are undifferentiated.

Everyone thinks that Chan is mysterious,

unfathomable, and beyond reach. But this is a limited view. But lines such as "By chance sleeping under a pine tree, a stone for a pillow. Time doesn't exist in the mountains, there's no more cold and there's no telling what year it is," and "The sound of a stream is the Buddha's teaching, the mountains a pure body" indicate that Chan is at hand everywhere. Chan is to be found within oneself, not outside. Nature is rife with it—look in front of you, bend down, pick it up, and there it is.

But there is an even greater misconception many people have, which is that they must go to a remote mountain retreat to practice meditation before they can attain enlightenment. But in fact, one need not leave people and go off to some ancient temple in the mountains to practice asceticism. Meditation and life are inseparable. Chan Master Kuaichuan said, "There is no need to go to the mountains to quiet the raging fires of the heart." All you have to do is quiet the fires of anger and hatred in your heart and what place won't be a cool and pleasing mountain landscape? A bustling public place can also be a place to practice Dharma. The story of the old woman who burned the hut describes a truly enlightened Chan master and not a dry-as-dust old monk who sits in meditation.[65] The true Chan master is concerned about others and lives a life of wit and humorous wisdom. In such a person's mind, the world is filled with vitality and all sentient beings possess the Buddha Nature. Everything is exactly that lively and natural.

Venerable Master Huineng said, "Chan means not being attached to external forms; concentration means having a composed mind." Chan meditation means that "the mind is unaffected by the world." Chan meditation keeps one's mind composed, it doesn't necessarily mean sitting quietly in meditation.

To practice Chan takes more than just sitting in meditation. And sitting in meditation does not necessarily mean that a person will attain Buddhahood. Take the question Chan Master Huairang of Bore Temple put to Mazu Daoyi, "If an ox pulls a cart but the cart doesn't move, should the ox be whipped or the cart?" The cart represents the body, and the ox our mind. This is why the Sixth Patriarch said, "Enlightenment comes from the mind, why bother sitting in meditation?" True Chan should be experienced in everything—walking, sitting, or lying down. It should be practiced in every way. True Chan meditation means that there is activity in tranquility and tranquility in activity, that activity and tranquility are one.

Although sitting isn't necessarily Chan, it is still very important and essential for beginners. This is especially true for most people today. If a person can sit for ten to twenty minutes and allow their active minds to regain some tranquility for a moment, they will feel the Dharma joy of serenity. This in itself will be like recharging their batteries.

Therefore, we ask, is Chan lively or rigid? Chan is lively, humorous, compassionate, and wise! Chan is like a pot of flowers, a painting, and seasoning in food. With Chan, life will improve and be more flavorful, allowing us to live more complete and artistic lives. With Chan, we will be able to act as the situation dictates, free from worry, free and easy in the vast world, subject to no troubles.

*T*he Perfection of Prajna-Wisdom:
Inner and Outer Completeness

According to the *Treatise on the Perfection of Great Wisdom*, the first five perfections are like the blind, and prajna-wisdom—the sixth perfection, is their guide. Prajna-wisdom is the basis of the six perfections, able to lead to the sea of wisdom via all means. Even most average people or adherents of other religions can practice the first five perfections—giving, upholding the precepts, patience, diligence, and meditation, but only with prajna-wisdom will charity be given with the essential emptiness of giver, receiver, and gift. Only with prajna-wisdom will the precepts be upheld actively as well as passively. Only with prajna-wisdom will patience be patience beyond unconscious patience. The lines, "The moon outside the window is always the same; it is different only when the plums blossom" can metaphorically describe how the perfections gain completeness only with prajna-wisdom, and only then can mundane dharmas be transformed into supramundane dharmas. Thus, the *Treatise* says, "Although the blind number in the tens of thousands, they will not be able to find their way into the city without a guide. The five perfections are just like the blind without a guide. Without prajna-wisdom, the Way cannot be fully cultivated."

Prajna-wisdom is the life and essence of the Mahayana teachings. As the *Treatise on the Perfection of Great Wisdom* says: "Mahayana is the same as the perfection of prajna-wisdom; the perfection of prajna-wisdom is the same as Mahayana." The importance of prajna-wisdom among the six perfections is paramount. Only with wisdom can a person realize that one's own nature is the intrinsic Buddha. And it was only because all the Buddhas of the three periods of time realized prajna-wisdom that they attained *anuttarasamyaksambodhi*. Venerable Master Yinshun once said, "Of what use is wisdom? With wisdom enlightenment is attained." The *Treatise on the Perfection of Great Wisdom* says, "All the Buddhas and bodhisattvas can benefit all. Wisdom is the mother that gives birth, raises, and teaches; the Buddha is a father to all sentient beings, and prajna-wisdom produces the Buddha. In benefiting all, prajna-wisdom is the grandmother to all sentient beings."

The Chinese term *bore* (般若) is a transliteration of the Sanskrit *prajna*, or "wisdom." It is a wisdom for practical use. Knowledge tells us that one is one and two is two. You might understand literature but that doesn't mean you necessarily understand chemistry. You might understand chemistry, but that doesn't necessarily mean that you understand physics. Newton learned about gravity by seeing an apple fall and Franklin discovered electricity, opening up the development of electricity as a science. These are examples of knowledge, and though knowledge may lead to understanding, it is still discriminatory, a worldly mix of confusion and enlightenment, which is never complete. But the enlightened nature of prajna-wisdom is to hear one and know ten, or "to know the many from the one." The enlightened nature of prajna-wisdom is the mutual realization of one's own nature and phenomena. In the *Diamond Sutra*

[*Vajracchedika Prajnaparamita Sutra*],[66] when Subhuti hears the wonderful Dharma, he is so touched that he weeps. After the Buddha realized perfect enlightenment he said, "Marvelous, marvelous! All sentient beings have the marks of the tathagata's wisdom and virtues. But they fail to realize it because they cling to deluded thoughts." These are the Buddha's words upon his enlightenment, a concerned sigh that all sentient beings are unable to integrate daily affairs and the Truth, and that they are unable to see the oneness of self and others as well as the oneness of mundane and supramundane dharmas.

From ancient times, many Buddhists have sought to recover their original face, overcoming ignorance and attaining enlightenment. Some spend a lifetime and are unsuccessful, while others achieve it in an instant. For example, Chan Master Lingyun Zhiqin attained enlightenment watching plum blossoms fall; the Bhiksuni Wujinzang realized her own treasury after seeing plum blossoms fall; Chan Master Yongming Yanshou realized his self nature hearing a tree branch fall; Chan Master Xiangyan

Zhixian uncovered his own precious treasury of suchness while hoeing the ground. These are some of the marvelous uses of prajna-wisdom.

The *Heart Sutra* (*Prajnaparamitahrdaya Sutra*)[67] says, "When Avalokitesvara Bodhisattva was practicing the profound *prajnaparamita*, he perceived the five skandhas as empty." This is enlightenment; enlightenment is prajna. Prajna is different from ordinary wisdom and even more different from knowledge, because there are pros and cons to ordinary wisdom and knowledge. Prajna is purity, truth, and goodness. Knowledge is arrived at through analysis of the exterior world; it is sought outside. Knowledge is good and bad, true and false. For example, the culture of science and technology invented the telephone, which is good for transmitting information, but which can also be used as a tool for committing crimes. Science invented gunpowder, which is good for opening a passage through the mountains, but which can be used to initiate violent wars leading to casualties.

In life, prajna is important. As the *Treatise on the Perfection of Great Wisdom* says, "*Prajnaparamita*, like light, can eliminate darkness and blindness. It is clean, beneficial, and brings tranquility; it can restore sight to the blind and set the wrongdoer on the right path. Prajnaparamita is the mother of all bodhisattvas; it can rescue the orphaned and the poor; it can extinguish the cycle of birth and death; it can proclaim the true nature of all dharmas."

Prajna is especially useful for understanding and extinguishing suffering, seeing emptiness, and being at ease. Life without prajna-wisdom will mean an absence of right views. This will make it easy to be vexed by externals, creating confusion, karma, and endless suffering on the wheel of transmigration. With prajna, one can light the lamp of one's own nature, attaining awareness of one's true life, and safely cross from this shore of samsara to the other shore of liberation. This, then, is the perfection of prajna-wisdom.

The Sutra on the Request by Manjusri

(*Manjusripariprccha Sutra*)[68] says, "All wrongdoings are like filth. Cleanse the mind with the waters of prajna-wisdom." Buddhists frequently chant the sutras, pay homage to the Buddha, listen to the Dharma, and do deeds of merit with the aim of cleansing the defiled mind. A clean mind is a precondition for prajna. Cleansing the mind of impurities is a must before the moon of bodhi will appear."

Is prajna, then, to be sought outside oneself or within? By seeking outside, you acquire scientific, philosophical, and other sorts of knowledge. But this is worldly knowledge that is unlike the enlightened prajna inside us. Prajna is like using one lamp used to light thousands of lamps—countless lamps with unobstructed illumination. Realize one's own nature and thousands of dharma worlds will enter the mind. With prajna, one's mind is capable of embodying the earth's vast mountains and great rivers, and all the mind's knotty problems will disappear like lacquer flaking away from a tub. Gone, all gone. How at ease!

Prajna is complete inner wisdom gained through "right views on dependent origination to realize that all dharmas are empty." Without prajna as a guide in life, it is like the story of the blind men and the elephant[69]—everything is unsure and unstable. With true universal prajna, the ugly is made beautiful and the dark becomes light. Therefore, if people can live and conduct themselves with prajna, life will become marvelous beyond compare.

Conclusion

The *Vimalakirti Sutra* (*Vimalakirtinirdesa Sutra*)[70] says, "His immeasurable wealth is used to sustain the poor and the helpless. He upholds the precepts to prevent others from transgressions. He practices patience to tame others from anger and hatred. He exercises diligence to help others overcome sloth. Concentrating in one-pointedness, he settles others' troubled thoughts. With prajna-wisdom, he educates the foolish."

There are many types of Buddhist practice, but the six perfections are the highest, unsurpassed method of practice and cultivation on the bodhisattva path of Mahayana Buddhism. Through giving charity a person can reap ten-fold by changing his stingy character. Upholding the precepts allows a person to purify the body, speech, and mind, altering bad behavior. Having patience can benefit oneself and others, changing one's bad habits of anger and hatred. With diligence everything is possible, and one can change one's old habit of laziness. With meditation comes stillness of body and mind and the way to change wild thoughts. With prajna-wisdom a person can look upon emptiness with ease, changing his foolish thoughts. If we seek enlightenment for ourselves and others, and if we seek to benefit ourselves as well as others, we need the six perfections. For only then will we find completeness and the path to Buddhahood.

The six perfections are exactly like six airplanes or ships carrying us toward a bright future.

1. Giving charity, the ship of "becoming rich."
2. Upholding the precepts, the ship of "safe and sound."
3. Patience, the ship of morality.
4. Diligence, the ship of success.
5. Meditation, the ship of calm mind.
6. Prajna, the ship of wisdom.

In today's world of science and technology, transportation is convenient and beneficial, but there are still traffic jams on the freeways and even many accidents. In the difficult ways of the world, if we have the spiritual course of the six perfections, the road to the future can be traveled with greater ease and accomplished according to one's wishes, even along the path of the bodhisattva to the land of the Buddha.

Are the six perfections for one's liberation alone, or for others as well? Are they for the enlightenment of others or oneself? Are they one's own, or do they belong to others? The six perfections are for others but also for oneself; they benefit others and also oneself. They are for the liberation of others and also for oneself; they belong to others and to oneself. The six perfections really are the Mahayana ship for the benefit and liberation of others as well as oneself.

*E*ndnotes

[1] **dependent origination:** *Skt.* "*pratitya-samutpada.*" Pali "*paticca-samuppada.*" This core principle of Buddhism means that all conditioned dharmas (phenomena) do not come into existence independently, but only as a result of causes and conditions, thus, no phenomenon possesses an independent self-nature. This concept is also referred to as "interdependence."

[2] **nirvana:** Pali "*nibbana.*" According to the *Sanskrit-English Dictionary*, the original meaning is "extinguished, calmed, quieted, tamed, or dead." In Buddhism, it refers to the absolute extinction of all afflictions and desires; in other words, it is the state of liberation, beyond birth and death. It is also the final goal in Buddhism.

[3] **samsara:** Also known as "*jatimarana,*" and means transmigration of birth and death. In detail, sentient beings die and are then reborn in the six realms of existence (the realms of heaven, human, asura, hungry ghost, animal, and hell). This kind of birth and death is continuous and endless, and is due to the karma of unwholesome deeds.

[4] **six perfections:** Also known as the six paramitas. "*Paramita*" in Sanskrit means "gone to the opposite shore," "transcendent," "complete attainment," "perfection in," and "transcendental virtue," according to the *Sanskrit-English Dictionary*. There are

several groups of perfections, such as the four perfections, the six perfections and the ten perfections. This paper discusses the second group. The last group, the ten perfections, includes the six perfections plus the perfections of the skillful means (*upaya*), vow (*pranidhana*), power (*bala*), and knowledge (*jnana*). These ten are the major practices that a bodhisattva should perform for attaining Buddhahood.

[5] **Nagarjuna:** Born in Southern India in the second ~ third century. He is the founder of the Madhyamika School (the School of Middle Way) and the author of many commentaries and treatises. His famous works include *Treatise on the Perfection of Great Wisdom*, *Treatise on the Middle Path*, the *Merits of Right Deeds Sutra*, and many more. Therefore, he was given the title of "the master of a thousand commentaries." He is a very important philosopher in Buddhism, and in Chinese and Japanese Buddhist history he is regarded as the founder of the eight major schools.

[6] *Treatise on the Perfection of Great Wisdom* (*Mahaprajna-paramita Sastra*): Ch. "*Da Zhidu Lun*" (T: vol. 25, no. 1509). A commentary on the *Sutra on the Perfection of Great Wisdom*, written by Nagarjuna and translated into Chinese in 402-205 C.E. by Kumarajiva, one of four great translators in Chinese Buddhist history. This treatise contains detailed interpretations of Buddhist doctrines, philosophies, illustrations, legends, history, geography, and rules of practice and the sangha. The main emphases are the philosophy and spirit of the bodhisattva path in Mahayana Buddhism and the practices of the six perfections.

[7] *Precepts of the Mulasarvastivada School* (*Mulasarvastivada Vinaya*): *Ch.* "*Genben Shuo Yiqie Youbu Pinaiye,*" translated into Chinese by Yijing, one of four great translators in Chinese Buddhist history. According to the *Sanskrit-English Dictionary*, "*mula*" means the root or foundation, and "*sarvastivada*" refers to the doctrine that all things in this world really exist. The Mulasarvastivadin is one of twenty schools in early Buddhism, which was divided from the Theravada School approximately 300 years after the Buddha entered parinirvana.

[8] **five groups:** In some English translations, it is also translated "the five classes" or "the five families." These groups are governors, thieves, water, fire, and prodigal descendants.

[9] *Collection of Great Treasures* (*Maharatnakuta Sutra*): *Ch.* "*Da Baoji Jing*" (T: vol. 11, no. 310). The title refers to the accumulation of great Dharma treasures and innumerable methods. The sutra focuses on the bodhisattvas' cultivation methods and predicting records of their progress in attaining Buddhahood. The methods include the teachings and practices of emptiness and the Pure Land and Tantric schools.

[10] **abhaya:** *Abhaya* means fearless, safety, security, peace, and removal of fear according to the *Sanskrit-English Dictionary*. The giving of *abhaya* is the third type of giving perfection. The person practicing the giving of *abhaya* helps others to feel safe, secure, and peaceful.

[11] *Lotus Sutra* (*Saddharmapundarika Sutra*): *Ch.* "*Miao Fa*

Lianhua Jing" or "*Fahua Jing.*" It is one of the most important sutras in the Mahayana tradition. The title means that the nature of the Dharma is as pure and undefiled as the white lotus flower. Its central message is that all sentient beings are able to attain Buddhahood. It is also a wonderful work of great literary merit. (*Fo Guang Encyclopedia and An Introduction to the Buddhist Canon*) In the *Chinese Buddhist Canon*, there are three versions: 1) Translated by Zhu Fahu in 286 C.E., titled Zheng Fahua Jing (T: vol. 9, no. 263), with 10 fascicles, 27 chapters. 2) Translated by Kumarajiva in 406 C.E., named *Miao Fa Lianhua Jing* (T: vol. 9, no. 26), with 8 fascicles, 28 chapters - this version is the simplest but most popular. 3) Translated by Jnanagupta and Dharmagupta, named *Tian Pin Miao Fa Lianhua Jing* (T: vol. 9, no. 27), with 8 fascicles, 27 chapters.

[12] **conditioned dharmas:** *Skt. "samskrta dharma." Ch. " youwei fa."* It indicates the phenomena arising from causes and conditions. The main characteristics of conditioned dharmas are arising, abiding, changing, and extinguishing. The conditioned dharma is impermanent, built upon the relation between cause and effect. And the fruit (effect) always follows it, therefore, sometimes it is known as "the dharma with fruit (effect)."

[13] **unconditioned dharmas:** *Skt. "asamskrta dharma." Ch. "wuwei fa."* The opposite of conditioned dharma: it is not dependent on causes and conditions for existence. It is apart from arising, abiding, changing or extinguishing. It is the absolute and usually an epithet for nirvana.

[14] **giving inappropriately:** Referring to giving materials that are acquired from an improper or illegal source, such as stealing or running an unwholesome business, or indicating weapons, guns, drugs, etc..

[15] *Sutra on the Principles of the Six Paramitas*: *Ch.* "*Dacheng Liqu Liu Boluomiduo Jing*," "*Liu Boluomiduo Jing*," or "*Liu Du Jing*;" translated into Chinese by Prajna, also named Bore Sanzang, in 788 C.E. (T: vol. 8, no. 261). This sutra describes how to protect the nation and how to practice the six perfections of the bodhisattva's cultivation. The ten chapters are: 1) Taking refuge in the Triple Gem, 2) mantra for protecting the nation, 3) awakening of the enlightened mind, 4) non-regression, 5) giving perfection, 6) perfection for upholding precepts, 7) perfection of patience, 8) perfection of diligence, 9) perfection of meditation, 10) perfection of prajna-wisdom.

[16] *Rain of Treasures Sutra*: *Ch.* "*Bao Yu Jing*" or "*Xian Shou Butuizhuan Pusa Ji*" (T: vol. 16, no. 660); translated into Chinese by Dharmaruci, also known as Bodhiruci, who was invited by the Emperor Gao of the Tang Dynasty in 693 C.E. to translate sutras. This sutra focuses on the ten teachings the Buddha spoke for the completion of the ten perfections and also for every kind of cultivation of the bodhisattva.

[17] *Merits of Right Deeds Sutra*: *Ch.* "*Fu Gai Zheng Xing Suoji Jing*" (T: vol. 32, no. 1671); translated into Chinese by Richeng. Its contents were collected and quoted from the sutras by Nagarjuna. The major purpose is to describe the right practices

and deeds such as the five precepts and the ten wholesome conducts that one should engage in to achieve virtues and merits.

[18] **Sutra on Upasaka Precepts** (*Upasakasila Sutra*): *Ch.* "*Youpose Jie Jing*;" translated into Chinese by Dharmaraksa (385-433) in 426 C.E. (T: vol. 24, no. 1488). This sutra discusses taking refuge in the Triple Gem and the five precepts. It explains the bodhisattvas' right intention, making vows, practicing and learning, upholding precepts, diligence, meditation, and wisdom.

[19] **seven limbs of enlightenment:** *Skt.* "*saptabodhyangani.*" This refers to seven kinds of practices to develop enlightenment. They are 1) mindfulness 2) investigation of dharmas 3) diligence 4) joyfulness 5) ease of body and mind 6) concentration and 7) equanimity.

[20] **the fruit of no outflows:** *Skt.* "*anasravah*" means "no outflows" or "without outflows." The fruit of no outflows indicates the state of liberation or those dharmas free from afflictions and leading to liberation.

[21] **eighty accessory marks:** *Skt.* "*asity-anuvyanjanani.*" The minor characteristics of Buddhas or bodhisattvas.

[22] **thirty-two excellent marks of a Buddha:** *Skt.* "*dvatrimsanmaha purusa laksanani.*" The remarkable physical characteristics possessed by a Buddha; they are the symbols of qualities attained at a high level of cultivation. They include a broad

tongue, a cone-shaped elevation on the crown of the head, a golden-hued body, and 29 more.

[23] **ten powers (*bala*) of the Tathagata:** *Skt. "dasa balani."* The Tathagata possesses various kinds of wisdom, along with which came ten kinds of power, which are knowing 1) right and wrong 2) the karma, cause, and effect in the past, present, and future lives of all sentient beings 3) all stages and forms of meditation 4) all sentient beings' faculties, tendencies, and powers 5) every sentient being's desires 6) the differences of all realms of existence 7) the results of conduct with outflows in the six realms of existence as well as the results of no-outflows practices 8) the transmigratory states of all sentient beings 9) the time of birth and death, the realms of rebirth, and all conditions of every sentient beings and 10) how to eliminate all afflictions.

[24] **four grounds of self-confidence** (*vaisaradya*): When Buddhas discourse upon the Dharma, they have confidence without fear. The four kinds of self-confidence are 1) having known all dharmas 2) having eliminated all outflows 3) having known all impediments on the path of cultivation and having no fears to confront them and 4) having shown the path leading to liberation.

[25] *Treatise on Arising the Mind of Enlightenment*: *Ch. "Fa Putixin Jing Lun;"* written by Vasubandhu, the author of the *Abhidharmakosa Sastra*, and translated by Kumarajiva (T: vol. 32, no. 1659). It is the commentary on the awakening of bodhicitta based on Mahayana sutras, commentaries and the

Abhidharma in Pali *Tripitakas*. It contains detailed explanations, interpretations, classifications and the terminologies with numbers (i.e. the Four Noble Truths, the Eightfold Noble Path, and the Three Dharma Seals).

[26] *Sutra of Cause and Effect*: *Ch. "Yin Guo Jing"* or *"Guoqu Xianzai Yin Guo Jing"* (T: vol. 3, no. 189); translated into Chinese by Gunabhadra (349-468); contains four fascicles. The first fascicle describes Sakyamumi Buddha explaining that in one of his past times, when he was names Shanhui Xianren, he made a great vow to practice the bodhisattva path in order to attain enlightenment and liberate other sentient beings. He then took refuge in Dipamkara Buddha, served him, and finally received a prophecy from him that he would attain Buddhahood after countless eons. The second, third and fourth fascicles describe the important events of Sakyamuni Buddha's life: his original birth as Prince Siddhartha, his leaving the royal palace to practice and develop wisdom, and his attainment of Buddhahood. The second to fourth fascicles can be called the biography of Sakyamuni Buddha.

[27] **three realms:** The realms where sentient beings reside and transmigrate: 1) the realm of sense-desires (*kama loka*), 2) the realm of form (*rupa loka*), and the realm of formlessness (*arupa loka*).

[28] *Sutra of Golden Light* (Suvarnaprabhasa Sutra): *Ch. "Jin Guangming Zui Sheng Wang Jing;"* translated into Chinese by Yijing (T: vol. 16, no. 665). One of three sutras for protecting the nation (the other two are the *Lotus Sutra* and *Karunikaraja*

Prajnaparamita Sutra). This sutra describes the virtues and merits of performing the Golden Light Repentance, as well as the belief of being protected by the Four Great Kings and the benefits of this kind of belief.

[29] **Sutra of the Teachings Bequeathed by the Buddha**: *Ch. "Fo Yijiao Jing"* (T: vol. 12, no 389); translated into Chinese by Kumarajiva. This sutra describes the Buddha's last teachings before he entered parinirvana. These teachings instruct the disciples to follow the *pratimoksa*, see it as the teacher, rely on it for guiding the five sense organs and attaining freedom.

[30] **Gatha of the Seven Ancient Buddhas**: *Ch. "Qi Fo Tong Ji;"* the verse of the seven ancient Buddhas' precepts for their disciples. In the time of the seven ancient Buddhas, the disciples were already pure and cultivated as they began to discourse teachings. Therefore, they did not need to set up additional disciplines or rules.

[31] **Sutra of the Bodhisattva Stages** (*Bodhisattvabhumi Sutra*): *Ch. "Pusa Dichi Jing"* (T: vol. 30, no. 1581); translated into Chinese by Dharmaraksa. Although it is called a "sutra," because of its contents it belongs to the classification of commentary. It describes the skillful means of Mahayana bodhisattvas' practice, divided into three parts: the beginning, the intermediate, and the ultimate. It also includes the Mahayana precepts.

[32] **slaying one to save a hundred:** In Buddhism, if ending one

person's life can save more lives, it can be understood and accepted. However, the person who pursues this action for giving others the security of life will still experience retribution for the karma and the effect of killing.

[33] **parajika:** In English, "the extremely unwholesome." It refers to the fundamental conduct that the bhiksu (male monastic) and the bhiksuni (female monastic) should not commit. Bhiksus have four *parajikas*, which are killing, stealing, lying, and sexual offense, and bhiksunis have eight *parajikas*, including the above four plus four more. The bhiksu or bhiksuni committing the *parajikas* will lose the qualification of monastic.

[34] *Five Part Vinaya* (*Mahisasaka Vinaya*): Ch. "*Wu Fen Lu*" (T: vol. 22, no. 1421); the precepts of the Mahisasaka School. The original Sanskrit version was acquired by Faxian Sanzang from Sri Lanka and translated into Chinese by Buddhajiva and Zhu Daosheng. It includes 251 precepts for the bhiksus and 370 precepts for the bhiksunis.

[35] *Flower Ornament Scripture* (*Avatamsaka Sutra*): Ch. "*Huayan Jing;*" Skt. "*Buddhavatamsaka Mahavaipula Sutra.*" It is one of the most important sutras in Mahayana Buddhism. There are three different versions (T: vol. 9, no. 278, no. 279 & no. 293) in the *Chinese Buddhist Canon.* 1) 60 fascicles, translated by Buddhabhadra (359-429); 2) 80 fascicles, translated by Siksananda (652-710); 3) 40 fascicles, translated by Prajna (734-?).

[36] **Long Discourses of the Buddha** (*Dirghagama*): *Ch.* "*Chang Ahan Jing*;" Pali "*Digha Nikaya*." Translated into Chinese by Buddhayasas and Zhu Fonian in 413 (T: vol. 1, no. 1). The Chinese version is composed of thirty sutras in four parts. The Pali version includes thirty-four sutras in three parts. The content slightly varies between the two versions due to interpretations and translations that sought to emphasize different schools of Buddhism.

[37] **Sutra Concerning Auspicious and Inauspicious [Conduct] Requested by Ananda**: *Ch.* "*Anan Wen Shi Fo Jixong Jing*;" translated into Chinese by An Shigao (T: vol. 14, no. 492). It teaches that if those who believe in the Buddha can study with a good teacher, diligently uphold precepts, and respect the Triple Gem day and night they will have no disasters in their life.

[38] **Abhisecana Sutra as Discoursed by the Buddha** (*Mahabhisekamantra Sutra*): *Ch.* "*Fo Shuo Guanding Jing* or *Da Guanding Jing*;" translated into Chinese by Srimitra (T: vol. 21, no. 1331). It contains twelve small sutras whose titles all begin the word "*Fo Shuo Guanding*" (abhisecana [sutra as] spoken by the Buddha).

[39] **Sutra on the Origins of Wholesomeness and Unwholesomeness**: *Ch.* "*Fo Shuo Fenbei Shan Er Suoqi Jing*;" translated into Chinese by An Shigao (T: vol. 17, no. 729). In this sutra, the Buddha teaches that if one does good deeds or upholds precepts, he/she will acquire five kinds merits or wholesome results for each good conduct. Conversely, the one committing bad deeds

or violating the precepts will gain five unwholesome results.

[40] *Sutra of the Sea Dragon King* (*Sagaranagarajapariprccha Sutra*): Ch. "*Hailong Wang Jing*;" translated in Chinese by Zhu Fahu (T: vol. 15, no. 598). In this sutra, the Buddha discourses upon the teachings of bodhisattva practice, such as the six perfections and ten virtues, to the Sea Dragon King at Vulture Peak. He also mentions that everyone, even if they are a woman, a sea dragon king, or an asura, can reach the state of liberation.

[41] **complete dentition:** The parts associated with the teeth, tongue and voice in "the thirty-two excellent marks of the Buddha": forty teeth, even teeth, white teeth, the wonderful taste for all foods, broad tongue, and voice like a Brahma's.

[42] *Ritual of the Triple Gem Refuge and Five Precepts Ceremony* (*Sanqui Wujie Zheng Fan*): The work of the vinaya by Master Jianyue.

[43] **ten wholesome conducts**: Indicating no killing, no stealing, no sexual misconduct, no lying, no duplicity, no harsh words, no flattery, no greed, no hatred or anger, and no ignorance.

[44] *Biography of Sakyamuni* (*Buddhacarita Sutra*): There are two versions in the *Chinese Buddhist Canon*: 1) Translated by Dharmaraksa, "*Fo Shuo Xing Zan*" (T: vol. 4, no. 192). 2) Translated by Baoyun, "*Fo Ben Xing Jing*" (T: vol. 4, no. 193). The statement in this paper is from the latter version. This is the representative work of Asvaghosa, and its references are from

the *Vedas, Upanishads, Mahabharata,* and *Ramayana.* It is also a wonderful work of ancient Sanskrit literature.

[45] ***Sutra of Forty-Two Sections***: *Ch. "Sishier Zhang Jing;"* translated into Chinese by Kasyapamatanga and Zhu Falan (or Dharmaraksa), (T: vol. 17, no. 784). It is the first sutra translated into Chinese. The content is concise and explains the basic doctrines of the early Buddhism. The emphases are on the explanations of the fruits of the monastics' attainment, the karmas of wholesomeness and unwholesomeness, the awakening of the mind, the abandonment of desires, the concept of impermanence, and the important meaning of becoming monastics and of learning the path.

[46] ***Sutra of the Right Mindfulness on the Dharma*** (*Saddharmasmrtyupasthana Sutra*): *Ch. "Zheng Fa Nianchu Jing;"* translated into Chinese by Bodhiruci (T: vol. 17, no. 721). The occasion for this sutra is non-Buddhists asking the new bhiksus questions about the karmas of the body, speech, and mind. The Buddha then discourses upon the methods of practicing right mindfulness of the Dharma. The Buddha clarifies the causes and effects of the three realms and the six paths of existence. It also focuses on the cultivation of monastics.

[47] ***Gradual Discourses of the Buddha*** (*Ekottarikagama*): *Ch. "Zeng Yi Ahan Jing."* Pali *"Anguttara Nikaya."* Translated into Chinese by Qutan Sengqie tipo (*Skt.* Gautama Sangha Deva?) It contains 52 fascicles and 472 sutras. Compared with other agamas, it is the most recent, and it embraces the Mahayana philosophy. It was named such because the Buddha gradually dis-

courses upon the methods of practice from one kind to eleven kinds.

[48] *Cultivating the Tree as the Bodhisattva's Practice Sutra*: *Ch.* "*Sihemei Jing*" or "*Pusa Dao Shu Jing*;" translated into Chinese by Zhiqian (T: vol 14, no. 532). This sutra describes the Buddha's discourses to the Elder's son Sihemei at Rajagra.

[49] *Garden of the Dharma and Pearl Forest* (*Fayuan Zhulin*): The work of Daoshi (?-683), finished in 668 C.E. (T: vol. 53, no. 2122). It is a kind of Buddhist encyclopedia that describes Buddhist philosophy, terminology, and "fashu."

[50] *Treasury of Truth* (*Dhammapada*): *Skt.* "*Dharmapada*;" *Ch.* "*Faju Jing*." The Chinese version (T: vol. 4, no. 210) has two fascicles and thirty-nine chapters, including 752 verses.

[51] *Commentary on the Sutra of the Teachings Bequeathed by the Buddha*: *Ch.* "*Yijiao Jing Lun*." The work of Vasubandhu; translated into Chinese by Zhendi (Paramatha or Kulanatha in Sanskrit), one of four great translators in Chinese Buddhist history (T: vol. 26, no. 1529).

[52] *Sutra on the Bodhisattva's Practice as Discoursed by the Buddha*: *Ch.* "*Fo Shuo Pusa Benxing Jing*." The Chinese version includes three fascicles and was recorded in the Eastern Jin Dynasty (318-420), but the translator is unknown (T: vol. 3, no. 155). The main emphasis of this sutra is on the practices of giving, diligence, and the ten wholesome conducts.

[53] **thirty-seven wings of enlightenment** (*bodhipaksika*): Thirty-seven kinds of practice leading to enlightenment: four applications of mindfulness on body, feelings, mind, and dharma, four right diligences, four bases of spiritual power, five faculties, five powers, seven limbs of enlightenment, and the Eightfold Noble Path.

[54] *Moon Lamp Samadhi Sutra* (*Srimalasimhanada Sutra*): *Ch. "Yue Deng Sanmei Jing"* (T: vol. 15, no. 639); translated into Chinese by Narendrayasas (490-589). This sutra describes the Buddha discoursing upon the teachings to Candraprabha (the Moon Light Bodhisattva). The teachings are how to achieve the five perfections of giving, upholding precepts, patience, and diligence through the mind of equality, protecting others, and no "poisons."

[55] **the blue lotus (*utpala*) is different than a log:** The lotus has the characteristics of softness and vitality; a log does not have these characteristics.

[56] *Lion's Roar of Queen Srimala Sutra* (*Srimalasimhanada Sutra*): *Ch. "Shengman Jing";* translated by Gunabhadra (394-468), (T: vol. 12, no. 353). This sutra is expounded by Srimala, the daughter of King Prasenajit of Sravasti. The main topics in this sutra are the one vehicle, the noble truths, dharmakaya, and the Buddha Nature. It also describes Srimala making ten promises and three great vows in front of the Buddha. This sutra is one of the representative sutras expounded by a layperson (similar to the *Vimalakirti Sutra*); it is also an authoritative text that a

woman can become a Buddha.

[57] *Treatise on the Awakening of Faith in the Mahayana*: *Ch.* "*Dacheng Qi Xin Lun.*" The work of Asvaghosa; translated into Chinese by Zhendi (T: vol. 32, no. 1666). It includes the philosophy of Mahayana Buddhism in terms of theory and practice.

[58] **Samantabhadra:** Samantabhadra Bodhisattva represents the transcendental practices and vows (ten great vows). He is usually depicted seated on an elephant with six tusks (symbolizing the six perfections).

[59] **three periods of time:** The past, the present, and the future.

[60] **ten directions:** Indicating east, west, south, north, southeast, northeast, southwest, northwest, the zenith and the nadir. The term refers to "all space or everywhere."

[61] **A descendent of National Master Yulin, with the enforcement of the Emperor Yongzheng, detached himself and was finally enlightened:** This story emphasizes that a person without discrimination in the mind practices diligently; this is one of the keys leading to liberation.

[62] *Inspiration for the Bodhicitta Pledge*: *Ch.* "*Quan Fa Putixin Wen.*" The work of Shixian (1686-1734), the Ninth Patriarch of the Pure Land School of Buddhism.

[63] *Treatise on the Completion of Truth* (*Satyasiddhi Sastra*):

Ch. "*Chengshi Lun.*" The work of Harivarman, the founder of the Satyasiddhi School; translated by Kumarajiva in 411-412 C.E. The subject of this sutra is the attainment of full understanding of the Four Noble Truths. This treatise explains that all phenomena in the universe have no substance; all will finally return to emptiness. And contemplating this principle will lead to a full understanding of the Four Noble Truths, the elimination of all afflictions through the practice of the Eightfold Noble Path, and finally to nirvana.

[64] **six dusts:** Indicating the six objects reflected by the six bases (sense-organs), then produce the six consciousnesses.

[65] **a dry-as-dust old monk who sits in meditation:** Some people think that meditation is only for aged monks and that it is difficult to apply in ordinary life. This phrase is an example of this kind of view.

[66] *Diamond Sutra* (*Vajracchedika Prajnaparamita Sutra*): *Ch.* "*Jingang Jin.*" Translated into Chinese by Kumarajiva, Bodhiruci and Zhendi (T: vol. 8, no. 235, 236 & 237). *Vajracchedika* means "the diamond that cuts through afflictions, ignorance, delusions, or illusions." *Prajnaparamita* is "the perfection of wisdom," or "the understanding that brings sentient begins across the sea of suffering to the other shore." (From the introduction of the *Diamond Sutra that Cuts Through Illusion*).

[67] *Heart Sutra* (*Prajnaparamitahrdaya Sutra*)**:** *Ch.* "*Xin Jing;*" translated by Xuanzang (T: vol 8, no. 251).

It is the shortest one and the summary of the wisdom sutras.

[68] **Sutra on the Request by Manjusri** (*Manjusripariprccha Sutra*): Ch. "*Wenshushili Wen Jing*;" translated into Chinese by Poluo (T: vol 14, no. 468).

[69] **the blind man and the elephant:** The blind man cannot see the elephant, he can only know the elephant by touching it. But each time he touches the elephant, he can only touch a part of it, so he only knows the elephant as the parts he touches, not the whole beast. Here, the eye is like prajna, which can lead us to see reality, which is symbolized by the elephant in the story. Therefore, without the eye (prajna) we cannot see the whole picture of the elephant (reality).

[70] **Vimalakirti Sutra** (*Vimalakirtinirdesa Sutra*)**:** There are three different Chinese translations of this sutra, completed by Kumarajiva, Zhiqian, and Xuanzang (T: vol. 14, no. 475-6); *Ch.* "*Weimoje Jing*," "*Weimo Jing*," and "*Wugou Cheng*," respectively. The main purposes of this sutra are to clarify the practicing methods of liberation that Vimalakirti has attained, and also to explain the practices of the Mahayana bodhisattvas and the virtues, which the layperson should fulfill.

ISBN 09715612-6-5